OHIO

a photographic journey

Text by Laura Watilo Blake

FARCOUNTRY
PRESS

Right: The crimson-patched longwing is one of many exotic butterfly species flitting around in the Butterfly House on South Bass Island.

Far right: Rock House, the only true cave in Hocking Hills State Park near Logan, is a 200-foot-long chamber carved over time by the wind and rain.

Title page: The John A. Roebling Suspension Bridge stretches over the Ohio River, linking downtown Cincinnati with Covington, Kentucky. When it first opened in the middle of the 19th century, the bridge became the longest of its type in the world. More than a decade later, Roebling, a civil engineer and pioneering designer, broke his own record with the Brooklyn Bridge in New York.

Front cover: Ash Cave, one of the most awe-inspiring features of Hocking Hills Park, got its name for the huge piles of cinders left behind by the area's earliest inhabitants. Although Ohio's largest recess cave impresses any time of the year, visit in the spring to witness the stunning waterfall that plummets 100 feet over the horseshoe-shaped rim.

Back cover: Few people, other than residents and their friends, ever get the chance to set foot on the intensely private Rattlesnake Island. It's been said the island got its name from the Ottawa tribe, who thought the two outcroppings, along with the serpentine shape of the larger landmass, resembled a rattlesnake with its rattles half submerged.

ISBN: 978-1-56037-704-7

© 2018 by Farcountry Press

Photography © 2018 by Laura Watilo Blake
Text by Laura Watilo Blake

Ohio State Buckeyes photo, page 60 © Jim Baron

For more information about our books, write Farcountry Press, P.O. Box 5630, Helena, MT 59604; call (800) 821-3874; or visit www.farcountrypress.com.

 Produced and printed in the United States of America.

22 21 20 19 18   1 2 3 4 5 6

This book is dedicated to my fellow travelers, friends, and family who had to wait and wait and wait while I got the right shot. A special thanks goes out to Chris and Kinley, who make the journey that much more worthwhile.

Left: Louis Bromfield made his name as a Pulitzer Prize-winning novelist, playwright, and screenwriter in the first half of the 20th century, but the dairy farm he bought in Ohio's Pleasant Valley became his true passion. While he pioneered soil conservation and self-sustaining farming practices at what is now called Malabar Farm State Park, famous friends came calling, including Humphrey Bogart and Lauren Bacall, who exchanged wedding vows in the main house in 1945. Today, the house and farm exist just as they did in Bromfield's time. Visitors can take a tractor-drawn tour of the property, see goats and cattle grazing on hillside pastures, and watch corn, wheat, oats, and hay swaying in the breeze.

Below: Bridle trails for horseback riding crisscross the hilly terrain of Laurelville's Spotted Horse Ranch. While the minimum riding age is eight years of age, younger children can ride ponies and see all kinds of farm animals from cows and sheep to more exotic species like the Asian water buffalo.

Above: Parasailing above Lake Erie offers a surprisingly peaceful view of the lake and Cedar Point Amusement Park in Sandusky.

Right: Cedar Point is one of the oldest operating amusement parks in the United States. More than three million people visit the park each season to ride its award-winning roster of roller coasters.

Above: At the Cincinnati Art Museum, Jim Dine's 12-foot-tall bronze sculpture of *Pinocchio* greets visitors with open arms.

Left: Hyde Park Square is an urban oasis in Cincinnati's oldest and hippest commercial district. A female statue, known locally as *Genevieve*, stands atop the tranquil Kilgour Fountain at the center of the shady park.

Above: Ohio has the world's largest Amish population, mostly centered in Holmes and Geauga Counties. Amish people eschew modern conveniences, including electricity, which is why you'll find clothes hanging on the line to dry on a frigid day.

Right: Amish children play in the schoolyard on a snowy day. Formal Amish education focuses on teaching hard work, ethical living, and submitting to church and God. When schooling ends in the eighth grade, boys hone farm skills or serve as apprentices in various trades, while girls help run family businesses or work outside the home as housekeepers, shop clerks, or restaurant servers until they marry.

Above: The Great American Ballpark is home to the Cincinnati Reds. The imaginary ballgame immortalized in bronze at the main entrance to the park depicts Reds alumni pitcher Joe Nuxhall, catcher Ernie Lombardi, and first baseman Ted Kluszewski.

Left: The Cleveland Indians team has had its ups and downs over the last century, but diehard fans always come out in droves to watch a game at Progressive Field in downtown Cleveland.

Right: A roadside stand near Mansfield displays freshly picked pumpkins for sale. The gourds grow especially gargantuan further south in Circleville—home to the Circleville Pumpkin Show's Giant Pumpkin Weigh-in, where past winners have reached almost 2,000 pounds.

Far right: A new day dawns in the Mohican Valley, where fog swirls over a field of soybeans—Ohio's leading agricultural export.

Below: Peifer Orchards' farm market, located just outside of Yellow Springs, displays apples for sale. The orchard has twenty-five varieties, which ripen to perfection between early September and late October.

Above: Cleveland's Franklin Castle, considered one of Ohio's most haunted houses, is a foreboding, four-story stone structure built in 1881 by Hannes Tiedemann, a German immigrant who made a fortune in banking. The unfortunate deaths of family members in the home have inspired more than a century of ghost stories.

Left: The stunning ruins of Squire's Castle sit on a sloping lawn in the North Chagrin Reservation of the Cleveland Metroparks. Built in the 1890s, the building was just the carriage house for a never-built country estate for Standard Oil Company co-founder Feargus B. Squire.

Right: The Scioto Audubon Park's rock-climbing wall is the largest free outdoor climbing wall in the country, set amid a 120-acre green space with plenty of recreational activities—and from the top, a view of downtown Columbus reveals itself.

Far right: Perkins Observatory, located at Ohio Wesleyan University in Delaware, gives astronomy enthusiasts the opportunity to peer into the depths of the universe.

Below: Built as a temple to the rock-music gods, the pyramidal Rock and Roll Hall of Fame, located on Cleveland's redeveloped North Coast Harbor, recognizes recording artists, producers, engineers, and other notables who have played an important role in rock and roll.

Above: Autumn's brilliant hues frame the Cleveland skyline from the upper section of Edgewater Park, a 147-acre urban lakefront park.

Left: Leaf peeping in Ohio is a nature lover's favorite autumn sport. Crisp, cool nights and warm, sunny days give way to fiery hues of yellow, orange and red. The Ohio Department of Natural Resources posts a foliage forecast on its website so you know exactly where to go in the state to catch the brilliant display.

Facing page: When the big orange ferry pulls in to Kelleys Island's port, its horn blows, the motor goes from a hum to a rumble, and gathering seagulls screech. The Kelleys Island Ferry shuttles cars and passengers between Marblehead and the Lake Erie island getaway every thirty minutes in the summer season.

Right: Graffiti carved into the soft Blackhand sandstone at Hocking Hills' Rock House dates to the early 19th century, but evidence of human occupation goes back 7,000 years, long before the state park's creation in 1924.

Far right: A monument in Dublin's Scioto Park pays tribute to Wyandot Chief Shateyaronyah, better known as Leatherlips. The Native American leader died in 1810 while defending his decision to keep the peace with white settlers rather than joining a coalition of tribes (led by Shawnee Chief Tecumseh) planning to fight against them.

Below: Wild bison last roamed Ohio's prairies more than two centuries ago, but overhunting got the best of them. America's national mammal has made a comeback in Galloway, home to a small herd that lives in an 18-acre enclosure at Batelle Darby Creek Metropark, which also has an interpretive center and hiking trails surrounded by grasslands.

Left: Marietta was founded by Euro-American pioneers coming to the Northwest Territory in the late 18th century. The original adventure town's location at the confluence of the Muskingum and Ohio Rivers made it ideal for industry and commerce, but now the rivers offer plenty of boating, kayaking, and canoeing opportunities, too.

Below: Ashtabula County boasts the most covered bridges in the state. The oldest of the bunch is believed to be the Mechanicsville Road bridge, which spans 156 feet across the Grand River near Geneva.

These pages: The Ohio Statehouse in Columbus took twenty-two years to complete after the ceremonial laying of the cornerstone in 1839. Most people are surprised that the building doesn't have a dome (far right), but it was never part of the original design in the first place. Based on the buildings of ancient Greece, the statehouse has a cupola (right) with a 29-foot-wide skylight that illuminates the interior rotunda. The color palette of French blue, straw yellow, and salmon, continues in the House Chambers of the Ohio General Assembly (below).

Above: More than a century ago, a farmhand investigating where water was disappearing into the ground, inadvertently discovered the largest cave system in the state, located in West Liberty. Ohio Caverns, as it is now known, opened ten days later to visitors who had to crawl through the tight space with a gas lantern. Enlarged over time, it's a lot easier to visit these days. Keep your eye out for the giant Crystal King, a 400-pound carrot-shaped stalactite that took more than 200,000 years to form.

Left: Ash Cave in Hocking Hills State Park has a wheel chair-accessible path that allows everyone to access the horseshoe-shaped recess cave reaching 700-feet wide and 100-feet deep.

Above: The Art Deco Lorain-Carnegie Bridge features four, two-sided sandstone pylons depicting eight *Guardians of Transportation*. Each 43-foot-tall figure holds a different vehicle in its hand, representing the evolution of ground transport from a stagecoach to a 1930s-era automobile.

Right: One of three iconic Cleveland signs, each with its own picture-perfect city backdrops, is located at North Coast Harbor. The other two can be found at the Abbey Avenue overlook and the upper section of Edgewater Park.

Facing page: Built in 1925 at the mouth of the Grand River, the Fairport Harbor West Breakwater Light is now a private home. The light, however, remains active—maintained by the U.S. Coast Guard for navigation.

Left: Ravenswood Castle provides one-of-a-kind overnight experiences in a secluded location in New Plymouth. Modeled after the great castles of Europe, the bed and breakfast has seven rooms, not to mention stand-alone cottages arranged to look like a medieval village.

Far left: Relics from the industrial revolution, these coke ovens were used to convert coal into coke, an important fuel for smelting iron ore. The ruins of the iron furnace and Belgian coke ovens can be found deep within Vinton Furnace State Forest in McArthur.

Below: Vinton County is home to the second largest swath of state forests in Ohio. Some of the backwood trails of the region are suitable for 4x4s and other all-terrain vehicles.

Right: Columbus' German Village isn't the only place to get a taste of Germany. The Hofbräuhaus, located in the Grandview neighborhood, has communal-style tables, giant portions of German fare, and of course, its famous beer that uses original recipes handed down by the Duke of Bavaria more than 400 years ago.

Far right: The vibrant murals of Columbus' Short North Arts District reflect the quirky character of the revitalized urban neighborhood, which is known for its galleries, shops, restaurants, and nightlife. Grant Wood's *American Gothic* inspired Steve Galgas and Mike Altman to paint a twist on the classic, located at the corner of North High and East Lincoln streets.

Below: Angelo Signorino, Jr., shares his passion for the beer-making process in the basement cave under Barley's Brewing Company in Columbus.

Above: A storm approaches Rattlesnake Island, an exclusive members-only island in the Bass Island archipelago in the western basin of Lake Erie.

Left: More than 150,000 inmates passed through the doors of the fortress-like Ohio State Reformatory in Mansfield during its ninety-four-year history as a working prison, and some never emerged again. Tour guides will recount tales of ghostly encounters as you wander through the free-standing multi-level cell block, solitary confinement, toilet room and showers, warden's office and living quarters, and the eerie chapel with a particularly scary spirit. Besides being featured on ghost-hunting television shows and music videos, the reformatory doubled as the prison in the movie *The Shawshank Redemption*.

Above: One part culinary arts studio and one part farm, the Glass Rooster Cannery in Sunbury uses upcycled materials in its whimsical outdoor art gallery, which includes a decorative leaning outhouse with a woodpecker door knocker.

Right: A fawn is one of many woodland animals that take shelter in the foliage of backyards bordering the Cleveland Metroparks—a 21,500-acre network of parks through the city that make up the "Emerald Necklace."

Far right: The county seat of Ross County, Chillicothe, was the first capital of Ohio. Adjacent to its historic downtown district, you'll find the 48-acre Yoctangee Park. The arched stone bridge that crosses the 12-acre horseshoe lake makes a perfect perch for trout fishing. The Ohio Department of Natural Resources releases approximately 100,000 rainbow trout into lakes across Ohio every spring.

Left: The sun rises over the Ohio River Valley as seen from Cincinnati's Eden Park lookout in one of the city's many hilltop enclaves. The popular 186-acre park also includes the Cincinnati Art Museum, Cincinnati Playhouse, and Krohn Conservatory.

Below: Lake Hope gets its name from an old mining town that now lies under the water's surface in almost the exact spot where this canoe slowly drifts on a peaceful early morning outing in Vinton County.

Above: The National Museum of the Great Lakes in Toledo preserves maritime history from early exploration of the Great Lakes to the environmental threats that challenge the waterways today. The largest artifact on display is the *Col. James M. Schoonmaker,* a restored freighter docked on the Maumee River just outside.

Facing page, left and top right: The Columbus Zoo and Aquarium is home to more than 10,000 animals representing more than 600 species from around the globe. Among other activities, you can watch a polar bear swim above your head, meet baby animals, or feed the giraffes.

Facing page, bottom right: Sly, the arctic fox, shows off her gorgeous winter white coat at the Cincinnati Zoo.

Below and right: Some of the innovative exhibits at The Toledo Zoo and Aquarium include encounters with endangered polar bears and underwater exploration in the aquarium, which has more than 3,000 sea creatures floating in 178,000 gallons of water.

Above: The mounded earthworks built by the Hopewell culture more than 2,000 years ago are shrouded in mystery. While little is known of their true purpose, some of the most well-preserved mounds can be found at Hopewell Culture National Historical Park in Chillicothe, where you can wander among them.

Facing page: The gazebo at Mohican State Park Lodge overlooks Pleasant Hill Lake in Loudonville.

Above: It's been more than 200 years since Commodore Oliver Hazard Perry prevailed over the British in the Battle of Lake Erie. Commemorating the battle, and the eventual peace that came after the War of 1812, Perry's Victory and International Peace Memorial towers 352 feet over the town of Put-in-Bay on South Bass Island.

Right: At Kelleys Island State Park, the morning sun illuminates tents pitched close to the edge of Lake Erie. Ferries offer frequent service to the island from nearby Marblehead and Sandusky.

Left: Like the spokes on a bicycle, five regional multi-use trails radiate from or near Greene County's Xenia Station, the largest cycling hub of its kind in the state. Riders from far and wide take to the trails each year. Eventually they will be able to travel all the way from Cincinnati and Cleveland on the Ohio-to-Erie Trail, which passes through Xenia via the Little Miami and Prairie Grass trails.

Far left: Chrisholm Historic Farmstead in Trenton provides a snapshot of rural Amish-Mennonite life in the late 19th century. Built in 1874, the brick home belonged to Samuel Augspurger and his family, leading members of the Anabaptist faith.

Below: Friendlier and softer than their llama cousins, alpacas are valued for their wool for making all kinds of clothing from socks to sweaters. One Fine Day Alpacas raises and sells alpaca, not to mention raw fiber, on its farm in Medina County.

Right: In winter, deer favor wooded areas sheltered from cold winds, like this forested valley behind Lake Erie Nature and Science Center in Bay Village.

Far right: Corn shocks sit on a snow-covered Amish farm in Holmes County. Once dry, the corn and shocks are often ground up for animal feed, used for animal bedding, or stored in cribs or silos.

Below: There are many designated sledding hills throughout the Cleveland metropolitan area, two of which are located in the Huntington Reservation of the Cleveland Metroparks.

Left: Bill Warren is the singing cowboy of Pony Tales Farm. He and his wife, Lorraine, raise rescue ponies at their North Ridgeville farm and use them for pony rides and other programs for kids between two and twelve years old.

Far left: Kayakers set off for a sunrise paddle on the scenic Deer Creek reservoir in Mt. Sterling. Kayaks and paddleboards can be rented at the Deer Creek State Park lodge.

Next pages: *Field of Corn,* often called "Cornhenge," is an unusual art installation in Dublin consisting of 109 concrete ears of corn. The site honors Sam Frantz, who developed several hybrid corn varieties at this location in the first half of the 20th century.

Below: Because fewer people are tent camping these days, the Ohio State Park system offers more comfortable camping alternatives that still encourage people to get outside. For example, Hueston Woods State Park in College Corner has a single yurt that comes with two futons, electricity, and a television with a DVD player.

These pages: The National Underground Railroad Freedom Center not only highlights the history of slavery and the path to freedom, but also sheds light on modern-day slavery, which lurks in the shadows—not just abroad, but also in our own cities. One of the highlights of the museum is a pair of quilts that document historical moments in African-American history as well as personal experiences in the life of artist Aminah Brenda Lynn (far left).

Right: The First Ladies National Historic Site consists of two downtown Canton properties: the childhood home of former first lady Ida Saxton McKinley (shown here) and the former National Bank Building, which houses the library and exhibits of artifacts from other first ladies.

Far right: The Rutherford B. Hayes Presidential Center consists of several buildings related to the life and political service of the country's 19th president. When he retired from office in 1881, Hayes returned home to Spiegel Grove, his sprawling wooded estate in Fremont. He and his wife are buried on the property, along with "Old Whitey," Hayes' beloved war horse.

Below: Oberlin Memorial Arch is considered the gateway between the city of Oberlin and college bearing the same name. Founded in 1833 by Reverend John Jay Shipherd and missionary Philo Stewart, Oberlin College has a long history of supporting social justice that began with its dedication to higher education for African-Americans and women. It's the oldest coeducational liberal arts college in the United States and the world's second oldest continuously operating coeducational institute.

Above and left: The football-shaped dome of The Pro Football Hall of Fame always commands the attention of those zipping by on Interstate 77 in Canton—the birthplace of the National Football League (NFL). The museum is a mecca for football fans, who can walk through the game's history-making moments with interactive displays and constantly changing exhibits, including the Hall of Busts, which grows each year as football greats are inducted into the Hall of Fame and immortalized in bronze (left).

Far left: Most often called "The Shoe" because of its horse-shoe shape, Ohio Stadium has been home to the Ohio State Buckeyes since 1922. The college football team represents The Ohio State University in the East Division of the Big Ten Conference. PHOTO BY JIM BARON

These pages: Four months after James A. Garfield's inauguration as the twentieth president of the United States, he was shot by a deranged gunman and died eighty agonizing days later from the wound. His final resting place is the James A. Garfield Monument, located in Cleveland's historic Lakeview Cemetery. Listed on the National Register of Historic Places, the monument is open daily from April through November.

Above: Kids are encouraged to discover plant and animal life through play in the Hershey Children's Garden at the Cleveland Botanical Garden.

Left: The Charles Herndon Galleries and Sculpture Garden are on Kelleys Island—Lake Erie's Emerald Isle.

Facing page: In 1992, sculptor James T. Madison made quite an impression with his topiary version of the post-impressionist painting *A Sunday Afternoon on the Isle of La Grande Jatte* by Georges Seurat. For the best view, head to the east side of The Topiary Park in Columbus and stand atop the hill next to the bronze-relief replica of the painting.

Below: Tulips bloom at the Cincinnati Botanical Garden.

Right: *The American Cape* by Kristen Visbal is one of more than 100 pieces of public art in Hamilton, known as the "City of Sculptures." The statue depicts the city's namesake, Alexander Hamilton, one of the founding fathers of the United States.

Far right: Three bronze deer sculptures placed in various locations along the Scioto River add a touch of whimsy to the Columbus skyline. The Scioto River takes its name from the Shawnee word for "hairy water." A local legend suggests that Native Americans found deer hair floating in the river when they first migrated to the area.

Below: The Cleveland Cultural Gardens took root on 250 acres of parkland donated to the city by John D. Rockefeller in 1897. Some of Cleveland's many ethnic groups are represented in the gardens along East Boulevard and Martin Luther King Jr. Drive, including this statue of Ukranian poet Larysa Petrivna Kosach-Kvitka (Lesya Ukrainka) that stands in the center of the garden, surrounded by cherry blossoms in the spring.

Above and below: Raven's Glenn Winery grows chardonel, vidal blanc, and noiret grapes on its West Lafayette property along the Tuscarawas River.

Left: In 2017, Middle Bass Island State Park reopened the historic Lonz Winery to visitors. Although most of the building had to be demolished, the front facade and iconic tower remain, along with the vault, which now displays artifacts from the winemaking process.

Far left: Built in 1866, this one-room schoolhouse in Dover is now home to The School House Winery.

Above and facing page: Strip mining forever changed the landscape of rural Guernsey County, but an innovative reclamation project converted 10,000 acres into what is now known as The Wilds—a private safari park and conservation center in Cumberland. The park is home to a number of rare and endangered animals from around the world, including cheetahs, greater one-horned Asian rhinos, Bactrian camels, Sable antelope, Grevy's zebras, and giraffes.

Top right: The Cleveland Metroparks Zoo has a five-acre habitat that mimics the African savannah for its herd of elephants to roam.

Right: A rare white tiger lounges in the sun at the Cincinnati Zoo and Botanical Garden—the second-oldest zoo in the United States. It opened in 1875, just fourteen months after the Philadelphia Zoo.

Above: A collection of log cabins from the late-18th and early-19th centuries make up Pioneer Village at Governor Bebb MetroPark near Okeana in Butler County.

Left: Dill growing around an old water pump at the Ohio Herb Education Center in Gahanna, known since 1975 as the herb capital of the state.

Far left: The Garden of Happiness, located at the center of historic Zoar Village, served all the members of the communistic society that settled here from 1817. The vegetables, fruit, medicinal herbs, and flowers grown in the garden contributed to the group's self-sufficient cash-free lifestyle that endured until 1898.

Above: After a half century of neglect, Cincinnati's Over-the-Rhine neighborhood has experienced a dramatic comeback as upscale investment drives the revitalization of one of the oldest and architecturally rich urban areas in the country. The area is home to some of the city's best local restaurants, breweries, and boutiques.

Right: Findlay Market—Ohio's oldest continuously operated public market—is ground zero for Cincinnati's culinary traditions. Some of the many vendors have gone on to run successful restaurants throughout the city, including waffle-maker Jean-Francois Flechet, who owns four Taste of Belgium bistros, while maintaining a stand at the market.

Far right: The River Queen sternwheeler passes under the John A. Roebling Suspension Bridge on the Ohio River.

Above: The unique village of Yellow Springs got its name from the iron-rich water that bubbles up from an underground aquifer within the Glen Helen Nature Preserve. Deposits of sediment give the surrounding rocks a yellow-orange hue.

Left: Cascading sixty-five feet over tiers of sandstone and underlying shale, Brandywine Falls ranks as one of the most popular attractions at Cuyahoga Valley National Park.

Facing page: The Old Baptist Church, a 19th century Protestant meetinghouse, is one of several historic buildings that make up Hale Farm and Village, an open-air living history museum located in Bath Township. The property has thirty-two historic structures on a farmstead that belonged to Jonathan Hale, a Connecticut farmer who migrated to the Western Reserve in 1810.

Above: One of the best ways to experience the dawn of aviation is by following in the flight path of the Wright Brothers, who created and perfected the first flying machine in the back of their Dayton bicycle shop. The National Aviation Heritage Historic Park pays tribute to the famous brothers and their impact on modern flight with a complex of buildings that includes a visit to the The Wright Cycle Company.

Right: The National Museum of the United States Air Force in Dayton is the largest and oldest military museum in the world. The multi-hangar facility houses everything from an original Wright Model B airplane to modern space-age rockets, not to mention a large collection of Presidential airplanes, including the SAM 26000, on which Lyndon Johnson was sworn in as president after the assassination of John F. Kennedy.

Far right: A replica Wright "B" Flyer, known affectionately as the "Brown Bird," lifts off from Dayton-Wright Brothers Airport, home to Wright "B" Flyer, Inc. An orientation flight is free for Honorary Aviator members of the non-profit organization that restored the plane.

Next pages: Many people who live by Lake Erie flock to its shores to watch the sun sink over the horizon on a summer night—as if performing an important pilgrimage. The Edgewater Beach House on Cleveland's near west side is an ideal spot, especially during the summer concert series on Thursday evenings at Edgewater Park.

LAURA WATILO BLAKE is the founder of eLBee Studio, a Cleveland-based visual media company. The internationally published, award-winning journalist, photographer, book author, and now independent filmmaker, made her directorial debut in 2018 with the travel documentary *Tripped Up*.

For more than a decade, Laura has produced content for a variety of media outlets, including *National Geographic Traveler*, *Trivago*, *Eater.com*, *Great Lakes Publishing*, *Edible Cleveland*, *Advanstar Communications*, *North Coast Media*, and *GIE Media*. In 2005, while completing her Master's in Media Management from Kent State University, Laura launched the travel website FarFlungTravels.com, which features stories and photography from around the globe. Since then, she has focused almost exclusively on travel journalism.

Her work has been recognized by the North American Travel Journalists Association and the Society of American Travel Writers, which also named FarFlungTravels.com the best travel website in 2013 in the central states chapter. In search of a good story, Laura's adventures have included hang gliding in Rio, traversing the Sahara Desert by camel, trekking in Bhutan, and dangling from the side of a Swiss mountain. But she's most often found around Ohio with camera in tow.